VIRGINIA WO

A Life from Beginning to End

Copyright © 2020 by Hourly History.

All rights reserved.

Table of Contents

Introduction
A Dysfunctional Home
Woolf and the Bloomsbury Group
The Making of a Modern Woman
Hogarth Press
Virginia Woolf and Impressionism
Mrs. Dalloway
Virginia Woolf's Mental Illness
Virginia and Vita's Love Affair
A Room of One's Own
The Waves
Woolf's Suicide and Beyond
Conclusion

Introduction

Virginia Woolf was born in a time of great change. The beginning of the twentieth century marked the end of the Victorian Era, and corsets and smelling salts were tossed to the wind. Women wanted more out of life than domestic servitude; they wanted to vote and earn their own living—a shocking sentiment at the time.

Virginia Woolf (born Virginia Stephen) was born in 1882 into a tremendously dysfunctional family. Her mother died when she was 13 years old. Her father, author Sir Leslie Stephen, tended to the education of his sons and sent them to university but saw no reason for his daughters to acquire an education. Ironically, it was the daughters, Virginia and Vanessa, who achieved fame and success. The sisters would always remain close.

Virginia—like Vanessa—was molested during her formative years, most likely contributing to her lifelong struggle with depression and mood swings. Although Virginia married Leonard Woolf in 1912, she was to remain ambivalent toward men all her life. Instead, she took on a female lover, Vita Sackville-West, and as a member of the free-thinking Bloomsbury Group, she advocated for sexual freedom.

Sadly, though Virginia achieved fame and success, happiness eluded her. Virginia sought answers through her books, the most famous of which is *Mrs. Dalloway*, but suicide was her final answer to questions she could never understand. On March 28, 1941, she filled her pockets with heavy stones and walked into the River Ouse, never to return.

Chapter One

A Dysfunctional Home

"If you do not tell the truth about yourself you cannot tell it about other people."

—Virginia Woolf

Adeline Virginia Stephen was born in London on January 25, 1882. Her parents were older than the average parent—her mother Julia was 36 years old, and her father Leslie close to 50 when they welcomed Virginia to the world. Their large house at 22 Hyde Park Gate was dim and shadowy, the atmosphere gloomy.

Virginia had three full siblings—one sister and two brothers. In addition to them, there were four half-siblings by both of her parents' previous marriages. The six-story house was extremely crowded, and Virginia's lifelong battle with depression began in this unhappy home. From the age of six, her half-brothers would reportedly visit her bedroom on a regular basis to molest her. In her later essay, *A Sketch of the Past,* Virginia points to the abuse as to why she felt ugly and ashamed throughout her life. In this regard, she would always feel close to and understood by her older sister Vanessa, who was also subjected to abuse by the half-brothers.

Even the good moments of Virginia's childhood ended in darkness. Her family spent summers in their house in St.

Ives by the sea. There, life was sunny and bright. Unfortunately, in 1895, their enchanting view was obstructed by the erection of the Porthminster Hotel, and the family never returned. Virginia summed up her disappointment with the words, "And St. Ives vanished forever." Virginia would long for the house at St. Ives for the rest of her life, with its beautiful gardens and view across the bay to the Godrevy Lighthouse. She was to use much of St. Ives in her later writing. The descriptions in her novel *The Waves* are memories of the idyllic seaside, and the Godrevy Lighthouse takes center stage in *To the Lighthouse*.

The same year that the family had to give up their seaside home, Virginia's mother Julia died of rheumatic fever. Julia, a model, had always been a great beauty but suffered from a sadness that her daughter inherited. Virginia was only 13 years old when she passed away, and she would mourn her mother for the rest of her life.

After Julia's death, the children's sole caregiver was their irascible father. Leslie was an educated man who arranged for his sons to receive a proper university education. Such a move, however, was not considered for the girls. He educated his daughters himself at home, and through Leslie, Virginia did receive more of an education than the average female of the time. She studied Greek and English classics, as well as history. Although Leslie disapproved of formal education for women, he did consider writing respectable and encouraged Virginia in this pursuit. Thus, both Virginia and her sister Vanessa spent a lot of time writing and painting during their formative years.

Still, Virginia was self-conscious throughout her life that her learning was not an official Oxford education that upper-class boys took for granted. As a girl, such a luxury was denied her. Later, Virginia was allowed to take a few classes in Greek, Latin, and German at the Ladies' Division of King's College. It wasn't the education her brothers received, but it was more than women could expect during those times.

After some years of illness, the aging Leslie died in 1904, when Virginia was 22 years old. Following her father's death, Virginia's half-brother George tried to take on a parental role for the girls and offered to provide them with an official coming out. Although for many girls such a debut would have been a special and memorable occasion, both Virginia and Vanessa were horrified at the idea. Even at a young age, neither of them showed signs of conforming to society's expectations.

Eventually, Virginia, Vanessa, and their brother Adrian found an apartment in Gordon Square in the Bloomsbury district in London. This new home was free of any parental restrictions, and the siblings did whatever they felt like. For Vanessa and Virginia, it was a time for gossiping, joking, and growing even closer.

Although Virginia lacked formal education, she was accepted as a teacher at the Morley College for Working Men and Women in London, where she taught composition and literature for two years. It gave her a firsthand look at the British educational system. She was disappointed that this working people's college spent so much time emphasizing popular courses instead of useful subjects that would lead to advancement in status and lifestyle. Her time spent here also served to show her the difference in education between the rich and the poor.

While Virginia was happy in London, these bright moments would be darkened when Vanessa became engaged to Clive Bell in 1906 and moved out. Two days before the proposal, their brother Thoby died. Lost, alone, and confused, Virginia wandered aimlessly through the streets of London. The double loss was difficult for her to accept.

Chapter Two

Woolf and the Bloomsbury Group

"Life for both sexes—and I looked at them, shouldering their way along the pavement—is arduous, difficult, a perpetual struggle. It calls for gigantic courage and strength. More than anything, perhaps, creatures of illusion, it calls for confidence in oneself. Without self-confidence we are as babes in the cradle. And how can we generate this imponderable quality, which is yet so invaluable, most quickly? By thinking that other people are inferior to oneself. By feeling that one has some innate superiority—it may be wealth, or rank, a straight nose, or the portrait of a grandfather by Romney—for there is no end to the pathetic devices of the human imagination—over other people."

—Virginia Woolf

The turn of the century was a time of major change in society as the old Victorian attitudes were set aside. Vanessa and her husband Clive were members of a new century and a new generation that fought against the restrictions of Victorian morality. They enjoyed an open marriage, and Vanessa soon became involved with artists Roger Fry and Duncan Grant. She and Duncan lived together despite his attraction to other men. Virginia meanwhile grew close to Fry, with whom she could discuss literature and poetry.

This growing network of young artists and intellectuals became known as the Bloomsbury Group, named after Virginia's living space, the Bloomsbury district of London, which was filled with wealthy elitists daring to be different. The so-called "Bloomsberries" were, for the most part, upper-middle-class artists and writers who proudly rejected mainstream ideas. They advocated for gay rights, women's suffrage, and sexual freedom at a time when the general population considered such ideas scandalous. They had grown up under the restrictions of the Victorian era and were proud rebels against societal conformity. Where their parents had been prudish, they were quick to deny any restrictions on their behavior—or their art. They were determined to change the world.

Virginia's brother Thoby, who attended Cambridge University until his death in 1906, had been instrumental in bringing the group together as he kept inviting his university friends for parties and discussions on controversial subjects. When asked why the group didn't meet in a public place, Vanessa cheerfully confessed, "The chief one seems to me to be that, as you say, we should have to eradicate politeness. We can get to the point of calling each other prigs and adulterers quite happily when the company is small and select, but its rather a question whether we could do it with a larger number of people who might not feel that they were quite on neutral ground."

The group was eager for discussions, but they were young and mischievous and wanted to have fun as well.

Thus, in 1910, Virginia, Adrian, Duncan Grant, Horace de Vere Cole, and two other friends dressed up in costumes and blackface and pretended to be Abyssinian royalty. They staged a visit to the Royal Navy in Weymouth, where Zanzibar's national anthem was played in their honor. The pranksters did a thorough inspection of the entire fleet without anyone noticing anything amiss. Afterward, Cole informed the newspapers of their charade, and the Royal Navy, furious and ridiculed, demanded Cole's arrest. No actual laws had been broken, however, and the Navy was left with nothing but a red face.

Following Vanessa's marriage to Clive Bell, Virginia and Adrian moved to Fitzroy Square in Bloomsbury, where the writers' group continued its meetings regularly on Thursday evenings. The artists' group met on Friday nights. Both nights, people began to appear at ten o'clock in the evening and remained until the early hours of the morning. The group was sustained by whiskey and cocoa. These get-togethers were popular, and the group kept growing. Virginia, still young and shy, didn't always participate in the debates, but she always listened.

Most members of the group were wealthy, and their critics accused them of being elitist snobs who merely condescended to the lower classes and the idea of equality. Since all male members of the group except Duncan were graduates of Cambridge University, it was difficult for outsiders not to regard them as exclusive. They were serious about their ideas, however—as serious as only the young can be.

Of course, the Bloomsberries were not above a bit of gossip, and the question of who Duncan was currently sleeping with was a favorite topic. An unconventional lifestyle was an integral part of being a member of the Bloomsbury Group, and instead of being discreet, they flaunted their indiscretions. Vanessa's marriage to Clive and lifelong affair with Duncan was accepted as modern and radically chic. It had excellent shock value. Vanessa, Clive, and Duncan were not the only threesome. Lytton Strachey was in love with Ralph Partridge, who, at the time, was married Dora Carrington. The concept of monogamy was scorned by most members of the group. These friends lived for drama and were not unlike the next anti-establishment rebels who were to appear decades later in the 1960s.

Virginia was just one of the successful writers. E. M. Forster wrote the classics *A Passage to India* and *A Room with a View* while a member of the Bloomsbury Group. Lytton Strachey became a popular biographer and author of books such as *Eminent Victorians* and *Queen Victoria*. Vanessa, her husband Clive, and her lover Duncan, meanwhile, were highly respected painters. Through their brother Adrian, Virginia and Vanessa also came into contact with the artist Pablo Picasso, whose Modernist, abstract paintings reflected much of the abstract nature of Virginia's writing. Vanessa acquired a Picasso sketch from the then relatively unknown artist for £4.

The Bloomsbury members would remain a supportive artistic group well into the 1930s. They helped many unknown artists enter their field and find success. By then, however, several prominent members had died. The group itself was no longer considered rebellious but within societal bounds, which defeated the entire reason for their existence. In addition, the looming war in Europe was occupying everyone's mind. The Bloomsbury Group came to an official end when Duncan Grant died in 1978 but had been mostly non-functional for decades.

Although the Bloomsbury Group worked diligently at being avant gard and equal, they associated with such renowned people as Pablo Picasso, poet Jean Cocteau, composer Eric Satie, and economist Maynard Keynes. Keynes, a bisexual man in a conservative Britain, found acceptance with the Bloomsbury Group. While the Bloomsbury Group challenged conventional thinking of conservatism, most of their ideas, such as equality and innovation, eventually turned mainstream in the twenty-first century and are now accepted as the norm.

Chapter Three

The Making of a Modern Woman

"The history of men's opposition to women's emancipation is more interesting perhaps than the story of that emancipation itself."

—Virginia Woolf

Although the Bloomsbury Group provided Virginia with plenty of new friends and acquaintances, Vanessa's marriage left Virginia feeling alone. She had no shortage of suitors, however, and Leonard Woolf, a civil servant and writer, had already proposed to her. They had first met when Virginia visited her brother Thoby at college. Virginia was beautiful (although she never believed so) and interesting, so it's no surprise that Leonard would become attracted to her. While he was stationed in Ceylon (modern-day Sri Lanka), a friend wrote to him and suggested he propose to Virginia. He didn't think his friend was serious but wrote back, "Do you think Virginia would have me? Wire to me if she accepts. I'll take the next boat home." Virginia, too, thought it was a joke and never replied.

Two years later, Leonard returned to England. Needing a place to stay, he rented a room in the house Virginia shared with her brother Adrian. They soon began to date.

Leonard continued to propose to Virginia, but she was reluctant. In a letter, she wrote, "As I told you brutally the other day, I feel no physical attraction in you. There are moments—when you kissed me the other day was one—when I feel no more than a rock. And yet your caring for me as you do almost overwhelms me. It is so real, and so strange."

While undecided about Leonard's proposal, Virginia dabbled with a group of people called the Neo-pagans. They were intellectuals and far left-leaning, attempting to achieve a utopian Socialist existence. Led by the poet Rupert Brooke, the members dedicated their mornings to writing. The rest of the day was spent frolicking through the woods, mostly barefoot, and swimming naked in the nearby rivers.

No doubt, both the Bloomsbury Group and the Neo-pagans filled a need for Virginia yet, feeling that she needed someone permanent in her life, she finally accepted Leonard's third proposal. They were married on August 10, 1912, when Virginia was 30 years old and Leonard 31. Their need for each other replaced the passion that their relationship lacked. Leonard quickly learned just how much Virginia disliked sex, something they both attributed to the sexual abuse she had suffered as a child. They hoped to have children, but because of Virginia's mental instability, her doctor advised against it. Instead, they had several dogs that replaced the children they were never to have.

By the time of Virginia and Leonard's wedding, Virginia had completed a draft of what would become her first novel, *The Voyage Out*. Because of her precarious mental state, it took her five years to complete the book, which was finally published in 1915. *The Voyage Out* is written in the stream of consciousness style that Virginia would adopt for all her novels. It deals with British colonialism, feminism, sexuality, and death—all sensitive topics in the early twentieth century. The story involves a group of voyagers on a journey of discovery. This mismatched group enables Virginia to satirize much about Victorian and Edwardian Britain. Like Virginia's later novels, *The Voyage Out* is written in a disjointed style with conversations that are about nothing specific.

The main protagonist is a young woman named Rachel Vinrace, who is traveling with her parents to South America by boat. Rachel has led a sheltered life due to her father's protectiveness. Onboard, she meets a couple who resemble the free-spirited Vanessa and Clive Bell. During the voyage, the innocent Rachel is also kissed by a Mr. Dalloway. She is confused but rather enjoys the incident. Virginia's own sexual history would serve as the basis for Rachel's confusion, and Rachel's transformation from sheltered to enlightened reflects Virginia's mental journey of discovery.

The Voyage Out was met with mixed reviews. E. M. Forster wrote that it was "a strange, tragic, inspired book whose scene is a South America not found on any map and reached by a boat which would not float on any sea, an America whose spiritual boundaries touch Xanadu and Atlantis." Literary scholar Phyllis Rose wrote, "No later novel of Woolf's will capture so brilliantly the excitement of youth."

Virginia Woolf, the author, was on her way.

Chapter Four

Hogarth Press

"Life is not a series of gig lamps symmetrically arranged; life is a luminous halo, a semi-transparent envelope surrounding us from the beginning of consciousness to the end."

—Virginia Woolf

Both Virginia and Leonard were progressive thinkers who spent many hours debating and arguing about current events. What their relationship lacked in passion, they made up in intellectual understanding. They soon joined the Fabian Society, a socialist group that later evolved into the Labour Party. Leonard was especially active in this group.

The Fabian Society propagated the new and progressive ideas of equality, which Virginia sincerely embraced. Later, she would refuse any public honors. When she was the only woman asked to deliver a lecture at Cambridge University, she declined. Such honors were in direct opposition to her idea of absolute equality.

In early 1915, Virginia and Leonard moved into Hogarth House, located near Richmond High Street. The house was large and a bit messy, the perfect workplace for both of them. While Virginia became the better-known writer, Leonard was publishing novels and essays long before she did. The year following their marriage, he published *The Village in the Jungle*, a description of his life in Sri Lanka. Other books quickly followed. Leonard also contributed regularly to the Fabian Society's publication, *New Statesman*.

In 1917, Leonard and Virginia founded Hogarth Press (named after their house), which published socialist brochures. It would also publish Virginia's future novels. Hogarth Press quickly established itself as a major publisher for modern writers such as T. S. Eliot, Roger Fry, and Gertrude Stein.

Around the same time, Leonard found a charming farm near Charleston that was ideal for Vanessa and Clive. The two moved in immediately. At this point, Clive was having an affair with the elegant Mary Hutchinson, and Vanessa brought along her lifelong lover Duncan Grant. Duncan helped renovate the farm building, even though he was occupied with his lover, David Garnett. The economist John Maynard Keynes would also become his lover. The Bloomsbury Group definitely practiced what they preached, and love affairs frequently became confusing.

No one in their circle thought this threesome—or foursome—was particularly odd. The Bloomsberries prided themselves, after all, in being modern. Vanessa soon found herself pregnant with Duncan's child and gave birth to a daughter, Angelica, on Christmas Day, 1918. Not to be outdone, David Garnett announced that he would marry Angelica at the proper time. They did begin an affair in 1938 and were married in 1942, much to the consternation of Duncan and Vanessa. Angelica and David eventually had four children.

Family relations were becoming and would remain complicated for Virginia. Still, she was always close to Vanessa. She was also close to Vanessa's two sons, Julian and Quentin. She took them into her home while Vanessa was busy taking care of Angelica. It was as close to being a mother as she would ever be. However, as Virginia tired easily, the situation did not last long.

The farm in Charleston became a hub of artistic activity. Painters painted, and writers wrote. Conversation was always vivid. Roger Fry was an enthusiastic contributor. As Virginia described it, "We discuss prose; and as usual some book is had out, and I have to read a passage over his [Fry's] shoulder. Theories are fabricated. Pictures stood on chairs." It was a haven of intellectualism.

In 1919, Virginia and Leonard purchased a small house in Sussex called Monk's House. This is where they stayed on weekends and during the summer months. The rolling green countryside near Sussex Downs appealed to Virginia. Like her childhood home by the sea, she reveled in the beauty and tranquility of nature. Vanessa's portrait of *The Lighthouse* hung prominently over the fireplace in the living room. Virginia wrote, "Monk House will be our address forever and forever." Much to her delight, Leonard built her a writing studio in the rear of the house. Later, following the publication of *Mrs. Dalloway,* Virginia added a luxury bathtub, where she spent her mornings reading her work out loud.

Chapter Five

Virginia Woolf and Impressionism

"The beauty of the world, which is so soon to perish, has two edges, one of laughter, one of anguish, cutting the heart asunder."

—Virginia Woolf

As an author, Virginia became part of a movement that was rethinking the aesthetics of the past and was eager to make its own mark. Impressionism demanded a new way of seeing things and a different way of expressing ideas. During their lifetime, many Impressionist artists were reviled for their anarchistic approach to art. Likewise, Virginia, being a Post-Impressionist and Modernist writer, was frequently misunderstood.

Bloomsbury member Roger Fry stated that writers during the Post-Impressionist period wanted "to make images which by the clearness of their logical structure, and by their closely-knit unity of texture, shall appeal to our disinterested and contemplative imagination with something of the same vividness as the things of actual life appeal to our practical activities." In other words, the aim of literature was to reflect real life instead of being a fantasy or illusion.

It is not difficult to determine how the Impressionist school of painting influenced the writers of the times. For example, one of the most important factors in Impressionist art is the use of light. Impressionist literature is meant to shed light on the inner life of a character instead of merely dealing with external events. That is the case in all of Woolf's writings. She was more interested in the feelings and emotions of her characters than in the actual events surrounding them. These events are seen through the subjective eyes of the characters.

Time is another critical element of Impressionism. Prior to the Impressionist period, paintings were simply a reproduction of objects and people. Impressionistic works created not only people and objects, but those people and objects were caught in a very specific moment of time, such as Renoir's dancers.

In Virginia's novel *To the Lighthouse* (published in 1927), the lighthouse is constantly changing as part of the story. For the characters, time is not linear but can take on a life of its own as it pervades and intrudes into people's minds. It doesn't have a beginning or logical end; instead, time is fragmented. According to Virginia, most writers of popular fiction were overly concerned with what happens on the surface, such as a logical progression of events, which she considered superficial.

In Virginia's short story *Kew Gardens* (published in 1919), she does not describe the characters strolling through nature at a specific time; rather, the details of the garden are seen through the flowers, in fragmented pieces of observations and recognition. The same style is used in her short story *The Mark on the Wall* from 1917. The narrator contemplates the mark in question with various fragmented impressions as the mind wanders from one thought to the next in no particular logical sequence.

While Virginia played around with different techniques in her short stories, her novel *Mrs. Dalloway* (published in 1925), with Clarissa Dalloway as the primary narrator, would become lauded as one of the best Modernist books of all time. Rather than an objective point of view, she describes the subjective inner experiences of her characters. The novel is about the characters' impression of events in bits and pieces instead of the events themselves. It is very much written in the stream of consciousness style of James Joyce.

In a letter to her sister Vanessa, Virginia wrote that "words are an impure medium." Her sister was a painter, and Virginia was a bit envious that her sister had, from her point of view, an easier task of expressing her ideas in colors and shapes. Virginia spent her entire life looking for the color equivalent of words.

Not so coincidentally, in *To the Lighthouse*, Lily Briscoe is an artist who captures her world in paint. When Virginia attempts to describe the deterioration of the lighthouse through the years, as well as the Ramsay family, without actually describing the lighthouse or the family, she does so mainly through allusions and thought fragments and colors. According to Woolf biographer Edward Bishop, "language is no longer to be used to create and communicate order but to bring one face to face with that region behind language where all is darkness and conjecture." In other words, art is the bridge between reality and subjective consciousness. Virginia was less concerned about the accuracy of reality than the impact of reality on the mind. As Lily exclaims of her paintings, "But this is what I see!"

Impressionist and Modernist literature is not about truth. Virginia never intended to present linear and logical facts. Instead, to her, literature was intended to reflect a specific moment of existence, something that can change time and time again, just as the mind can keep forever changing. In this, Virginia Woolf emulated the artists of her time whom she admired and who were able to capture an important moment on canvas.

Chapter Six

Mrs. Dalloway

"Mrs. Dalloway is always giving parties to cover the silence."

—Virginia Woolf

Virginia's most famous novel, *Mrs. Dalloway*, was published on May 14, 1925, by Leonard's and Virginia's own publishing company, the Hogarth Press. Virginia first had the idea for the novel following a visit with the socialite Lady Ottoline Morrell in 1923. Lady Ottoline regularly hosted the Bloomsbury Group, but she was regarded as a caricature and frequently mocked due to her social pretensions. She appeared as the foolish Hermione Roddice in D. H. Lawrence's *Women in Love* and was thought to be the inspiration for Lawrence's title character in *Lady Chatterley's Lover*.

Following a party at Lady Ottoline's house, Virginia noted in her diary, "A loathing overcomes me of human beings—their insincerity, their vanity—A wearisome and rather defiling talk with Ottoline last night is the foundation of this complaint... I want to bring in the despicableness of people like Ottoline: I want to give the slipperiness of the soul. . . . I want to give life and death, sanity and insanity; I want to criticize the social system, and to show it at work, at its most intense."

Mrs. Dalloway became one of the most acclaimed novels of the twentieth century. The entire novel recounts a single day in the life of wealthy Clarissa Dalloway following the end of World War I. Clarissa spends the day preparing for a party she is hosting, and the novel is a glimpse into the minds of several of the characters. The story does not evolve in any linear order. Instead, time shifts haphazardly back and forth in a stream of consciousness between several characters who describe societal changes created by the war. The scenes, not always related, provide a momentary insight into a character's thoughts. Whatever dialog exists tends to be inner dialogue.

As Clarissa wanders through London shopping for her party, her mind wanders back and forth in time. She contemplates her marriage to the reliable and dull Richard Dalloway when she might have had the dashing Peter Walsh. Clarissa is anxious about her role in London's upper-class society.

Meanwhile, Septimus Smith, a war veteran, sits in a park with his wife, Lucrezia. Septimus has frequent thoughts and hallucinations about a friend and comrade who died in the war. Lucrezia believes society will judge her because of Septimus' illness. By the end of the day, Septimus will have committed suicide. That evening at the party, Clarissa learns of Septimus' suicide. Although she doesn't know him, she admires his courage.

In terms of style, *Mrs. Dalloway* is frequently compared to James Joyce's novel *Ulysses*. Interestingly, Virginia did not like Joyce's work. According to her, "I finished Ulysses, and think it is a mis-fire. Genius it has I think; but of the inferior water. The book is diffuse. It is brackish. It is pretentious."

The shift in time is extremely relevant in *Mrs. Dalloway*. While the novel takes place in the present, the characters' thoughts continuously shift to the past. For Clarissa, it's her childhood home in Bourton. Those thoughts repeatedly mingle with thoughts of the present. Septimus also lives very much in the past, specifically the war and his fallen friend. Throughout the day, conversations with his dead soldier friend flow through his mind. In the novel, Big Ben looms over London and loudly announces each new half-hour as the characters are reminded of time and loss by the sound of the bell cutting through the stream of consciousness. Time moves on, whether they wish it or not.

Virginia, who struggled with mental illness herself, criticizes society's view and treatment of depression in *Mrs. Dalloway*. Septimus' doctors do not take him seriously and are extremely dismissive. His wife ignores his struggle and states that "Septimus was not ill. Dr. Holmes said there was nothing the matter with him."

Another theme in *Mrs. Dalloway* is the emerging post-World War I feminism. Clarissa both fulfills her expected role as the wife of a politician while finding a personal creative outlet in her many parties. Her friend from school, Sally Seton, used to smoke cigars and display unladylike behavior to shock people. At the party, however, it is clear that Sally has turned into the type of housewife and mother expected by bourgeois society. Their relationship hints at bisexual feelings. Clarissa remembers their shared kiss in school as one of her life's most magical moments.

Virginia weaves in criticism of the British Empire and colonialism into *Mrs. Dalloway* as well. Britain occupied territories in Asia, India, and Africa. This changed after World War I. Hundreds of thousands of British soldiers died in World War I, causing the country to suffer tremendous financial losses and loss of status. Still, the British elite attempt to continue life as if nothing had changed. This is especially implied in society's indifference to the suffering of Septimus, which is easier to ignore than to acknowledge. This separatism is enhanced by the fact that Clarissa and Septimus never actually meet in the novel. Virginia makes it clear that pretending nothing is wrong is more important to the British upper classes than finding solutions to the existing problems.

Almost every character at the party is concerned with class distinction. Clarissa herself does not invite a poor relative to her party to spare herself the embarrassment. Less wealthy guests feel tremendous envy toward Clarissa because of her wealth. Still, Clarissa feels isolated and is not sure how to communicate her thoughts and feelings. The purpose of the party is to get closer to her upper-class guests. However, talking about flowers and children are as deep as the conversations get.

Meanwhile, the character of Septimus very deliberately refuses to communicate and discuss the trauma inside of him. This, of course, makes it impossible for his wife to understand what he is going through. Rather than reveal his inner turmoil, Septimus commits suicide. While Clarissa does not know him, she learns of his death at the party. To her, Septimus' act of suicide is an act of communication.

Chapter Seven

Virginia Woolf's Mental Illness

"I am made and remade continually. Different people draw different words from me."

—Virginia Woolf

Virginia suffered from mental illness all her life. She was depressed a lot of the time and felt like she was going mad. Concentrating often became difficult. Throughout her life, she made several unsuccessful suicide attempts. In modern medical jargon, she would be considered manic-depressive or bipolar, but even that diagnosis needs to be questioned. Virginia was a complicated woman who struggled with life and not always succeeded.

Her first mental breakdown occurred when she was 13, following the death of her mother. She suffered her second major breakdown in her early twenties after her father died. More breakdowns would follow at irregular intervals. These breakdowns were totally disabling and required her to stay in bed. No medication was available in those days to alleviate the symptoms as psychiatry was still in its infancy. Virginia was institutionalized on several occasions, which was the only known treatment for mental illness.

When she was manic, she couldn't stop talking until she became incoherent. When she was depressed, she couldn't function. She frequently blamed herself for her mental frailties, which only made things worse. In fact, Virginia's family had a history of serious mental dysfunction. Her brother Thoby had shown signs of mental disturbance before his death. Her sister Vanessa suffered from periods of depression. Their father and grandfather both suffered from depression, as well. A cousin was placed in an asylum.

From all appearances, gloom and doom had haunted Virginia's family for generations. She was sexually abused by her half-brother, and one might assume that her sister and half-sisters were likewise molested. Most of the family was creative and artistic by nature. Virginia's mood swings made her seem both shy and elated, depending on the circumstances. Her manic episodes were her creative periods. When she was depressed, she was unable to create anything.

Although Virginia is remembered for her gossipy nature and brilliant conversations, she never felt comfortable with people outside of her social strata. Her appearance bordered on the eccentric. Until her death, she lived in daily fear of her next depressive episode. Her fear was reasonable; statistics show that up to 95 percent of manic-depressive patients suffer from recurring episodes.

Although she reportedly chose lovers of both sexes, Virginia was definitely frigid with men. There is some conjecture that some of her depressed moods during her marriage were a convenient way to help her deal with the physical pressures of her marriage. As one friend stated,

"Virginia would take refuge in nervous stress to escape her marital problems." To his credit, Leonard always remained devoted and loved Virginia in spite of her problems.

Virginia genuinely attempted to understand what was happening to her. Mostly, she made use of her characters in an attempt to bring logic to an illogical situation. This is especially true of the character of Mrs. Dalloway, whose inner turmoil reflected Virginia's own jumbled and confused thoughts.

Virginia's psychiatrist had her institutionalized in a private home for ladies with a nervous disorder several times. These times coincide with the death of her father and her marriage to Leonard in 1912. Clearly, change made her uneasy. The last two institutionalizations were in the countryside, where her doctor hoped she might respond more positively to treatment for her depression and insomnia. However, deprived of her family, friends, and reading material, Virginia found the situation unbearable. As she wrote to Vanessa, "I shall soon have to jump out of a window."

When she returned home, she made another suicide attempt but was found in time. She spent the next two years trying to recover. There was another suicide attempt, but a second psychiatrist, Dr. Maurice Craig, determined she was not ill enough to be committed again. It was a slow and difficult upward crawl. Her friends noticed a permanent change in her behavior from which she would never recover. Writing was her lifeline. She wrote, "The only way I keep afloat is by working. . . . Directly I stop working I feel that I am sinking down, down. And as usual, I feel that if I sink further I shall reach the truth."

Virginia's diagnoses were always vague, and this made it more difficult for her to cope.

Chapter Eight

Virginia and Vita's Love Affair

"As long as she thinks of a man, nobody objects to a woman thinking."

—Virginia Woolf

Although Virginia and Leonard shared a strong bond and would remain together until the end, Virginia would meet a person who would introduce her to a whole new type of love affair at age 40.

Vita Sackville-West was ten years younger than Virginia. They were very different people. Vita came from a prominent aristocratic family, while Virginia was a Bohemian writer. Like so many members of Virginia's circle, Vita had a history of same-sex relationships. Although she had married diplomat Harold Nicolson in 1913, both she and Harold were far more interested in same-sex relationships. Like Virginia's sister, Vita and Harold enjoyed an open marriage. Vita saw herself as having two separate personalities: one was feminine and submissive and attracted to men while the other was hard and aggressive and attracted to other women.

Virginia and Vita first met at a party in late 1922. Virginia had at this point not even begun her major novel,

Mrs. Dalloway. In a letter to her husband, Vita wrote, "I simply adore Virginia Woolf, and so would you. You would fall quite flat before her charm and personality . . . I've rarely taken such a fancy to anyone, and I think she likes me. At least, she asked me to Richmond where she lives. Darling, I have quite lost my heart."

When it came to romantic relationships, Virginia was almost virginal. Her growing attraction to Vita confused her. She sensed a certain danger, which only added to the arousal. Vita was aware of Virginia's fragile state of mind and allowed the relationship to grow slowly. While Virginia lived a simple life, Vita lived a life of luxury and indulgences, which impressed Virginia even though she had spent her life promoting classless equality.

Within a few years, they each became the most important person in the other's life, although Vita had other female lovers. Both their husbands were understanding bystanders to the relationship without any injection of jealousy. Especially Leonard, always concerned about Virginia's mental and physical health, was supportive of anything that might help brighten his wife's mood.

During these years, Virginia wrote her semi-autobiographical novel, *Orlando* (published in 1928), based on her relationship with Vita. It was a groundbreaking story about gender that has stood the test of time and remains relevant in the twenty-first century. The book is written as a fantasy about lesbianism and bisexuality rather than an actual account thereof, a fine distinction which may have spared it from any censorship. While the Bloomsbury Group embraced same-sex relationships, it was still a shocking topic to the rest of the world that was holding onto gender stereotypes.

Like most of Virginia's writings, *Orlando* is filled with shifting characters and fluctuating time periods. Even femininity and masculinity become fluid as the character of Orlando falls asleep as a man and wakes up as a woman. The character asks the reader to imagine what would happen if we weren't restricted by our gender identity.

At the beginning of the novel, Orlando is a dashing British nobleman living in sixteenth-century England. A friend to Queen Elizabeth I, he is very popular with her ladies but refuses to do the expected thing and marry one of them. Instead, he falls in love with a Russian princess named Sasha. Sasha harshly rejects him and goes back to her homeland.

Dejected, Orlando returns to his castle and spends his time writing sad love poems. When he reveals his poetry to his poet friend Nicholas Greene, Nicholas publishes the poems as a kind of literary spoof. Feeling betrayed, Orlando burns all his poems except for one, which he calls *The Oak Tree*. He is so disappointed in Nicholas that he insists he is "done with men." He spends his time redecorating his castle, but it is a fruitless effort since he has removed himself from human companionship and there is no one to invite to his newly redone home.

As he continues to work on *The Oak Tree*, Orlando notices a beautiful lady strolling outside of his window. He invites her in for tea. The woman is a Romanian Archduchess named Harriet. Orlando wants an uncomplicated, short relationship, while Harriet is after a commitment. Orlando decides to leave his castle and travel to Constantinople.

In an unexplained turn of events, Orlando wakes up as a woman. She is now in her thirties. After a visit with some local gypsies, she returns to England. There, she finds that being a woman has considerable disadvantages. Orlando gets sued for owning a castle; at that time, women were not permitted to own any property. Harriet arrives unexpectedly at the castle; then, she also changes gender and turns into Archduke Harry.

Harry declares his love, but Orlando isn't interested. She goes to London to party with other aristocrats but finds them lacking. While the male Orlando was unable to live up to the expectations of manhood, female Orlando is equally unable to meet societal expectations of womanhood. There is no description of time passing; however, as the clock strikes midnight, Orlando finds herself in the nineteenth century in the Victorian Era.

The Victorian Era is, of course, known for its repressive attitudes, especially toward all matters sexual. Orlando struggles against the limitations but soon gives up and gets engaged to a sea captain named Marmaduke Bonthrop Shelmerdine. Orlando finishes her poem, *The Oak Tree*, and takes it to a publisher. The publisher and literary critic in question is her old friend, Nick Greene, who promises to publish it.

At the end of the novel, Orlando is calling out to her husband. Unhappy, she lies down on the ground and informs Shelmerdine that she is dead. It's not her body that has died, but her spirit. Death is not depicted as something to be feared but rather as a way to become revitalized. This foreshadows Virginia's own thoughts on death and suicide.

Orlando was published on October 11, 1928. On that day, she had her original manuscript, bound in leather, delivered to Vita. Reviewers were aware that the novel was based on Virginia's and Vita's personal relationship and didn't know quite how to handle such a sensitive subject matter. The public, however, avidly bought enough copies to ensure a bestseller.

Chapter Nine

A Room of One's Own

"Women have served all these centuries as looking glasses possessing the magic and delicious power of reflecting the figure of man at twice its natural size."

—Virginia Woolf

Published in 1929, *A Room of One's Own* is an essay based on Virginia's lectures at Newnham and Girton colleges for women. Virginia had always resented the fact that being a woman had deprived her of a college education. Now, she was doing her own lecturing.

In this essay, Virginia takes a feminist stance and argues for education and economic independence for women. This was not the norm at the time when most women were expected to be housewives. For female writers, she stated, it is necessary to have a room of own's own, away from the world of male dominance. The book also contains one of her most famous quotes, "One cannot think well, love well, sleep well, if one has not dined well." This was a reference to the excellent meals served at men's colleges, while women's colleges had to make do with meals of lesser quality.

It is interesting to note that while *A Room of One's Own* is a cry for feminism and freedom for women, Virginia was not writing about all women. The old class distinction frequently discussed by the Bloomsbury Group still existed for her. Virginia was specifically writing about women of genius—not ordinary women. This criticism is often made against Virginia, and it is a legitimate one. As a feminist, did she consider the lot of a salesgirl, secretary, or nurse?

A Room of One's Own is not written in Virginia's usual fragmented style. It is a linear presentation of arguments for women's rights. Economic freedom for women, she claimed, is a major priority that would lead to other freedoms. Virginia discusses that history has invariably been male-dominated and that women have always been marginalized. As a writer, she refuses to accept that women are less talented writers than men. She points out that women are provided with a lesser education and not taken as seriously. At the time, women were not permitted to attend certain universities. They were expected to marry and let their husbands take control while they kept busy with household chores and raising children. The essay appeals to female writers to write on any topic, not just "women's issues."

To her own surprise, the book sold well. The topic was dear to many younger women who desired greater freedom.

Chapter Ten

The Waves

"Alone, I often fall down into nothingness. I must push my foot stealthily lest I should fall off the edge of the world into nothingness. I have to bang my head against some hard door to call myself back to the body."

—Virginia Woolf

During the late 1920s, Virginia wrote her innovative novel *The Waves*. She had by now celebrated her fiftieth birthday, and this stage of her life caused her to reflect upon the years past.

In *The Waves*, the six main characters are on a journey of self-discovery. They are totally obsessed with death and have dwelled on this morbid topic their entire lives. The reader follows the characters from childhood to old age. To emphasize the theme of death, the character of Rhoda commits suicide.

Another character, Bernard, understands how dependent he is on other people—a situation that closely resembled Virginia's own. He realizes how he changes in relation to whoever is present. It's as if he were an empty vessel to be filled by others. His world is one of inner consciousness rather than one of objective outer reality. Throughout *The Waves*, the characters struggle to define themselves, which they do through their relationships with others. Bernard articulates this struggle most clearly. He realizes that who he is dependent on who surrounds him—his words and thoughts change in relation to his companions. His consciousness is his only reality. He totally rejects the concept of an outer reality. It is the mind that creates his world. This includes the flowers he sees, which would not exist if he didn't see them.

The character of Neville, who also defines himself by the opinion of others, attempts to create a better consciousness to reduce his dependence on others. Louis does the same things. Rhoda is the most fragile of the group. She feels empty of all thoughts and has difficulty relating to others.

All the characters yearn for greater substance and meaning. Life is constantly changing for them, and they try to adapt to the real world and its randomness mostly through art. Art is seen as outside of time, something permanent. Surely this was Virginia's own life-long struggle. While Bernard searches for meaning in the paintings at a museum, he remains frustrated and longs for a simpler language. Words are insufficient, but so are the shapes and colors of paintings. He desires to provide conscious meaning to these external objects.

As the characters try to make sense of their thoughts and lives, they cannot control death and their mortality. The realization that death is an objective reminds them that there is a reality and that they are a part of real time. Their plan is to face death as a fact of life. One can see Virginia's struggles with suicidal thoughts in how her characters think about death. Only one character, Rhoda, succumbs to the lure of death. Considering the fact that Virginia had suicidal thoughts throughout her life, this character was probably a very real part of her.

By the time *The Waves* was published in 1931, Virginia was a known and successful author. Critics and readers alike enjoyed the novel, and almost 7,000 copies were sold during its first month.

Following the publication of *The Waves*, Virginia and Leonard took a trip through Europe in 1935. By this time, they no longer had the company of the Bloomsberries to entertain them, many of whom were either dead or had become what they once despised. Virginia was rich and successful. Keynes was now a major economist. Forster was a celebrated author. Vanessa and Duncan were respected painters. The former rebels had run out of ideas to rebel against. They themselves were now the dreaded bourgeois.

With Hitler amassing power, this was a very dangerous time to be traveling, especially since Leonard was Jewish. Every German town through which they drove had massive Nazi propaganda posters on display. In Bonn, their car was stopped by troops, but luckily, they escaped without harm. In her diary, Virginia complained of their nervousness and being forced to act obsequiously. The couple was relieved to reach the border. The world was indeed changing, and not for the better.

Chapter Eleven

Woolf's Suicide and Beyond

"Against you I will fling myself, unvanquished and unyielding, O Death!"

—Virginia Woolf

The outbreak of World War II was especially difficult to handle for a devoted pacifist such as Virginia. In 1941, she plunged into a deep depression—the likes of which she had never suffered before. The Germans were destroying her beloved London, and her biography of the dearly departed Roger Fry (published in 1940) had received lukewarm reviews. She spent much of her time unable to work. To make things even worse, Leonard was filled with a burst of patriotism and joined the Home Guard. She continuously criticized him every time he wore his uniform. Her thoughts were obsessed with death.

During this time, she was struggling with her final novel, *Between the Acts,* which was published after her death. Like *Mrs. Dalloway,* the story unfolds in a single day. A small village has organized a pageant just before the beginning of World War II. As in most of Virginia's work, gender plays a major role in the novel. Bartholomew Oliver represents selfish male imperialism, while his sister, Mrs.

Swithin, represents the selfless local community. Both feel tremendous uncertainty about the future. Like in *Mrs. Dalloway,* the story shifts in a fragmented style between several minds, especially on the topic of expected gender roles. Men are expected to build empires while women are relegated to caring for the home—these ideas as explored randomly and in no particular order.

During the pageant, airplanes can be heard overhead, indicating that Britain is entering into a time of war. Life as the citizens knew it will change forever. Death is not far away. Virginia alludes to death (a topic that was obviously consuming her mind) in subtle ways. A housemaid remembers a woman committing suicide in a pond. She wonders about the afterlife and the woman's fate. Is she now a ghost? Mrs. Swithin meanwhile takes in the beauty of the surrounding, its mountains, greenery, and waterfalls. She comments, "That's what makes a view so sad and so beautiful. It'll be there when we're not."

Shortly after she completed *Between the Acts*, Virginia Woolf succeeded in her final suicide attempt. On March 28, 1941, wearing a heavy coat with pockets filled with rocks, she walked into the nearby River Ouse. She drowned herself, a final act she had carefully planned by choosing the time and means of death.

In a note to Leonard, Virginia confessed to hearing voices and to her fear of another bout of madness—one from which she might not recover. Her note ended with, "Everything has gone from me but the certainty of your goodness. I can't go on spoiling your life any longer. I don't think two people could have been happier than we have been."

Unfortunately, the River Ouse swept her body away. No one knew exactly what had happened or where she was. Her body was not discovered for three weeks during which time her family became increasingly frantic. When she was finally found, the *Associated Press* printed in bold headlines, "Mrs. Woolf's Body Found."

There was no funeral. Virginia was cremated, and her remains were buried under one of the two intertwined elm trees in her backyard, which she had nicknamed "Virginia and Leonard." Leonard marked the spot with a stone tablet engraved with the last lines from her novel *The Waves*: "Against you I fling myself, unvanquished and unyielding, O Death! The waves broke on the shore."

Virginia's final novel, *Between the Acts*, was eventually edited by Leonard and published July, several months after her death. This was an incredibly challenging time for Leonard, Virginia's husband of almost 30 years. In his biography, he wrote, "They said 'Come to tea and let us comfort you.' But it's no good. . . . I know that she is drowned and yet I listen for her to come in at the door."

The pain only grew worse. Virginia's last letter to Leonard was made public, and a month after Virginia's death, the wife of the bishop of Lincoln wrote to the *Times*: "Sir, — I read in your issue of Sunday last that the coroner at the inquest on Mrs. Virginia Woolf said that she was 'undoubtedly much more sensitive than most people to the general beastliness of things happening in the world today.' What right has anyone to make such an assertion? If he really said this, he belittles those who are hiding their agony of mind, suffering bravely and carrying on unselfishly for the sake of others. Many people, possibly even more 'sensitive,' have lost their all and seen appalling happenings, yet they take their part nobly in this fight for God against the devil." This callousness was devastating to Leonard. But journalism, then and now, could be cruel.

Luckily for Leonard, there was some joy to come. A year following Virginia's death, he met a woman named Trekkie Parsons. She was an expert lithographer, and Leonard hired her to illustrate several books for Hogarth Press. Within a year, he was in love with her. Trekkie could not have been more different from Virginia. She lived joyfully in the present. She cared nothing for politics and new ideas. For Leonard, perhaps this was a breath of fresh air.

Trekkie never divorced her husband, but she divided her time equally between him and Leonard. She redecorated Leonard's home and very much acted like a wife. Leonard meanwhile continued his efforts on behalf of the Fabian Society and the Labour Party.

Conclusion

Eighty years following her death, Virginia Woolf remains a major influence in literature. Undoubtedly, she is one of the most important literary figures of both English literature and feminist literature. Virginia Woolf is still studied today, a time when gender roles and equality are crucial topics. Her influence has spread to many modern writers who have been inspired by her novels.

In the early 1960s, Edward Albee, an American playwright, wanted to use Virginia's name in his play, *Who's Afraid of Virginia Woolf?* Leonard was happy to grant it and even went to see the play in London. He enjoyed it. *Who's Afraid of Virginia Woolf?* is still performed today.

Michael Cunningham's novel *The Hours* is a fictionalized version of how *Mrs. Dalloway* affected three generations of women. Cunningham brings the reader into Virginia's mind and thoughts up to her final suicide. He changes some of the character names; Clarissa Dalloway, for example, becomes Clarissa Vaughan. Thoughts and viewpoints are as fragmented as the original. Cunningham's novel was published in 1998 and promptly won a Pulitzer Prize. *The Hours* was adapted for film in 2002, with Nicole Kidman as Virginia Woolf—a role for which Kidman received an Oscar.

Life in Squares was a BBC series about Virginia Woolf and focused on her relationship with the Bloomsbury Group and her sister, Vanessa. It emphasized both the artistic accomplishment of the sisters as well as the sexual escapades of the Bloomsberries.

Room magazine, which used to be called *Room of One's Own*, is a feminist journal established in 1975, giving women of all gender persuasion a voice.

Much has changed for women and the LGBTQ community since Virginia Woolf wrote her novels. However, without a doubt, she would be surprised how much has remained the same. Were she alive, there is no doubt Virginia Woolf would continue her fight. As she once wrote, "Lock up your libraries if you like; but there is no gate, no lock, no bolt that you can set upon the freedom of my mind."

Printed in Great Britain
by Amazon